Weekly Reader Books presents

Handling Your Ups and Downs

A Children's Book about Emotions

by

Joy Wilt

Illustrated by Ernie Hergenroeder

Educational Products Division
Word, Incorporated
Waco, Texas

Contents

Introduction   **5**

Chapter 1
Feeling Up (Comfortable Feelings)   **21**

Chapter 2
Feeling Down (Uncomfortable Feelings)   **37**

Chapter 3
Handling Your Downs   **113**

Conclusion   **125**

Introduction

Handling Your Ups and Downs is one of a series of books. The set is called **Ready-Set-Grow!**

Handling Your Ups and Downs deals with human emotions and can be used by itself or as a part of a program that utilizes all the **Ready-Set-Grow!** books.

Handling Your Ups and Downs is specifically designed for children four to eight years of age. A child can either read the book or have it read to him or her. This can be done at home, church, or school.

Handling Your Ups and Downs is designed to involve the child in the concepts that are being taught. This is done by simply and carefully explaining each concept and then asking questions that invite a response from the child. By answering the question, it is hoped that the child will personalize the concept and, thus, integrate it into his or her thinking.

It isn't at all difficult to handle comfortable feelings because they make us feel good about ourselves and life in general. There is nothing more pleasurable than feeling happy, loved, and respected. We receive and experience these feelings without hesitation.

On the other hand, we avoid feelings that make us uncomfortable, and often repress or reject those feelings. Repressing or rejecting uncomfortable feelings is extremely unhealthy because when feelings are repressed or rejected they are not dealt with. Feelings that are not dealt with eventually hinder a person from growing and living a healthy, productive life.

Even though uncomfortable feelings are a necessary part of life, they are difficult to cope with, especially if one does not know how to handle them. This is precisely why <u>Handling Your Ups and Downs</u> proposes a specific four-step procedure for children to follow when they experience uncomfortable feelings. The goal of this book is to equip children with the skills they need to handle their ups and downs.

Handling Your Ups and Downs

9

Every person sometimes. . .

feels up.

And every person sometimes. . .

feels down.

11

When a person feels up. . .
he or she experiences comfortable (good) feelings.

Everyone likes comfortable feelings.

They can help a person. . .

have fun and enjoy life.

13

When a person feels down. . .
he or she experiences uncomfortable (bad) feelings.

People don't like to feel bad. But sometimes uncomfortable feelings can be good for a person.

Uncomfortable feelings can make a person. . .

do things that need to be done.

Uncomfortable feelings can also make a person...
grow and change for the better.

And, uncomfortable feelings can help a person. . .

appreciate his or her comfortable feelings.

Even though a person might want to feel up all the time. . .

sometimes he or she
is going to feel down.

It is normal and healthy for a person to have both ups and downs.

Chapter 1

Feeling Up
(Comfortable Feelings)

Love is feeling cared for and being valued by others.

Love is an emotion that makes people feel comfortable.

24   Acceptance is feeling liked and respected by others.

Acceptance is an emotion that makes people feel comfortable.

Security is feeling safe.

Security is an emotion that makes people feel comfortable.

Pride is feeling good about oneself and the things that one does.

Pride is an emotion that makes people feel comfortable.

I KNOW IF I TRY HARD ENOUGH, I CAN LEARN TO RIDE THIS BIKE.

Confidence is feeling that you can do things on your own.

30

Confidence is an emotion that makes people feel comfortable.

Happiness is feeling joyful and contented.

Happiness is an emotion that makes people feel comfortable.

Love
Acceptance
Security
Pride
Confidence, and
Happiness

. . . are all feelings that make people feel comfortable.
They are feelings that make people feel good.

Can you think of other feelings that make people feel good?
List them here:

_____

_____

_____

_____

_____

The best way to handle comfortable feelings is to be thankful
and enjoy them whenever you experience them.

Everyone likes comfortable feelings. They can help a person have fun and enjoy life.

Chapter 2

Feeling Down
(Uncomfortable Feelings)

Anger is feeling mad. Anger is an emotion that makes people feel uncomfortable.

39

Hurting other people or not taking care of their things is not a good way to handle anger.

Telling someone that you are angry, explaining why you are angry, and trying to do something about what is making you angry. . .

are good things to do when you are mad.

THINK

Have you ever felt angry?   Yes ☐ No ☐

List some things that make you angry:

_____

When was the last time you got angry?

_____

What did you do? How did you handle your anger?

_____

REMEMBER

Getting angry is OK. But when you are angry, try not to:

hurt other people, or
mistreat other people's things.

It is best if you:

> tell someone you are angry,
> explain why you are angry, and
> try to do something about what is making you
> angry.

Also, it is OK to:

> cry,
> scream,
> yell,
> jump up and down, or
> hit or kick things that cannot be damaged
> (like pillows, punching bags, or beds) as
> long as you do not bother anyone else
> while you are doing it. This might mean
> that you will need to go outside or into
> another room and close the door while you
> are angry.

Guilt is the feeling of having
done something wrong.

Guilt is an emotion that makes
people feel uncomfortable.

44

But sometimes . . .

guilt makes a person do what needs to be done.

Lying, pretending that nothing happened, or trying to hide what you have done wrong is not a good way to handle your guilt.

Admitting that you did something wrong, saying you're sorry, and (whenever possible) trying to make up for what you have done...

are all good things to do when you feel guilty.

THINK

Have you ever felt guilty? Yes ☐ No ☐
List some things you have done that made you feel guilty:

_____

When was the last time you felt guilty?

_____

What did you do? How did you handle your guilt?

_____

REMEMBER

When you have done something wrong, it is normal for you to feel guilty. But when you feel guilty, try not to:

   lie,
   pretend as if nothing happened, or
   hide what you have done wrong.

It is best if you:

   admit that you did something wrong,
   say that you are sorry, and
   try, whenever possible, to make up for what you did.

Also, it is understandable for you to:

   cry,
   feel ashamed and embarrassed,
   not want everyone to know about what you did, or
   find it hard to admit that you were wrong and say you
      are sorry.

Jealousy is wishing that you were like another person or wishing that you had what another person has.

Jealousy is an emotion that makes people feel uncomfortable.

But sometimes . . . jealousy makes a person do what needs to be done.

Saying mean things about other people, hurting them in any way, or trying to compete with them is not a good way to handle jealousy.

Telling someone you are jealous and asking for help or attention are good things to do when you are jealous. Other good things to do are:

Try not to compare yourself with others. Concentrate on the fact that you are a special person and unlike any other person. Think about the fact that you have many things that no one else has.

THINK

Have you ever been jealous?   Yes ☐   No ☐

List some people of whom you have been jealous:

_____

When was the last time you felt jealous?

_____

What did you do? How did you handle your jealousy?

_____

REMEMBER

When it appears that someone is getting more attention
or has more than you, it is normal for you to be
jealous. It is also normal to be jealous of a person
who seems to be better than you. But when you are
jealous, try not to:

> say mean things about the person,
> hurt the person in any way, or
> compete with the person of whom you are
>   jealous.

54

It is best if you:

> tell someone about your jealousy,
> ask for help or attention,
> try not to compare yourself with others,
> think about the fact that you are a special person
>   and unlike anyone else,   and
> think about the fact that you have many things that
>   no one else has.

Also, it is normal for you to:

> be jealous of your brothers and sisters,
> want to be the best at everything (even though you
>   can't be because no one is best at everything), or
> want to have the most (even though you can't because
>   that wouldn't be fair).

Grief is feeling sad. Grief is an emotion that makes people feel uncomfortable.

But sometimes . . . grief makes a person do what needs to be done.

Pretending that nothing is wrong or hiding your sadness is not a good way to handle your grief.

Admitting that you are sad and talking about your grief are good things to do when you are sad.

59

THINK

Have you ever felt grief?   Yes ☐ No ☐

List some things that made you sad:

_____

When was the last time you felt sad?

_____

What did you do? How did you handle your grief?

_____

REMEMBER

When something sad has happened, it is normal for you to feel grief. But when you feel grief, try not to:

    pretend that nothing is wrong or
    hide your grief.

It is best if you:

    admit that you are sad, and
    tell someone about your grief.

Also, it is understandable for you to:

    cry,
    want to be alone,
    wish that whatever is making you sad hadn't
      happened, or
    want to forget about what is making you sad.

Loneliness is feeling all alone. Loneliness is an emotion that makes people feel uncomfortable.

But sometimes . . .

loneliness makes a person do what needs to be done.

Thinking that no one would want to play with you or be your friend, refusing to make friends, or trying to get someone to notice you by being bad is not a good way to handle loneliness.

Admitting that you are lonely, finding someone to play with, and making friends are all good ways to handle loneliness.

65

THINK

Have you ever felt lonely?　　Yes ☐　No ☐

List the times when you felt lonely:

_____

When was the last time you felt lonely?

_____

What did you do? How did you handle your loneliness?

_____

REMEMBER

When there is no one around for you to talk to or play with, it is normal for you to feel lonely. But when you feel lonely, try not to:

think that no one would want to play with you or be your friend,

refuse to make friends, or

get someone to notice you by being bad.

It is best for you to:

    admit that you are lonely,
    find someone to play with, or
    make friends with someone.

Also, when you are lonely, it is understandable for you to:

    feel rejected,
    be bored, or
    need to be noticed.

Rejection is feeling that you are unwanted. It is feeling that you are not liked or accepted.

Rejection is an emotion that makes people feel uncomfortable.

But sometimes . . . rejection makes a person do what needs to be done.

THEY DON'T WANT ME BECAUSE I'M NO GOOD AT BASKETBALL. I'M NO GOOD AT ANYTHING; THERE'S NO USE EVEN TRYING.

Believing that you are no good, or giving up and not trying is not a good way to handle rejection.

Remembering that no one person is liked by everyone and can be good at everything is a good way to handle rejection.

Other good things to do are:

Think about your good points,
Do the things you do well,

I CAN'T PLAY BASKET-BALL, BUT I CAN PLAY THE TRUMPET.

Hang around people who like and accept you,
Try not to be around people who do not appreciate you.

THINK

Have you ever felt rejected?   Yes ☐ No ☐

List some people who you feel reject you:

_____

_____

_____

When was the last time you felt rejected?

_____

What did you do? How did you handle being rejected?

_____

REMEMBER

When other people do not appreciate you or accept you, it is normal for you to feel rejected. But when you feel rejected, try not to:

> believe that you are no good,
> give up, or
> stop trying.

It is best if you:

remember that no one person is liked by everyone,
remember that no one person can be good at everything,
think about your good points,
do the things that you do well,
hang around people who like and accept you, and
try not to be around people who do not appreciate you.

Also, it is understandable for you to:

wonder about yourself and your capabilities after you
  have been rejected,
not like or want to be around people who reject you, or
want to prove that you are OK to the people who
  reject you.

Humiliation is feeling embarrassed or put down. Humiliation is an emotion that makes people feel uncomfortable.

But sometimes . . . humiliation makes a person do what needs to be done.

Putting down, getting back at, or hurting the people who have humiliated you is not a good way to handle humiliation.

Ignoring the put-downs and walking away are the best ways to handle being humiliated.

THINK

Have you ever been humiliated? Yes ☐ No ☐
List some times when you were humiliated:

_____

When was the last time you were humiliated?

_____

What did you do? How did you handle your humiliation?

_____

REMEMBER

When you have been embarrassed or put down in front of
other people, it is normal for you to feel humiliation. But
when you are humiliated, try not to:

put down anyone else,
 get back at the people who humiliated you, or
 hurt the people who have humiliated you.

It is best for you to:

    ignore the put-downs, and
    walk away.

Also, when you have been humiliated, it is understandable
for you to:

    not want to see or be around the people who were
      there when you were humiliated, or
    not want to remember or think about humiliating
      moments.

Frustration is feeling uptight and discouraged. Frustration is an emotion that makes people feel uncomfortable.

But sometimes . . .

frustration makes a person do what needs to be done.

Breaking or not taking care of things is not a good way to handle your frustration.

THIS TOY FRUSTRATES ME, DAD. CAN YOU HELP ME WITH IT?

Slowing down, trying again at another time, or getting someone else to help is a good way to handle frustration.

83

THINK

Have you ever been frustrated?   Yes ☐   No ☐
List some things that frustrate you:

_____

_____

_____

When was the last time you got frustrated?

_____

What did you do? How did you handle your frustration?

_____

_____

REMEMBER

Being frustrated at times is normal. But when you are
frustrated, try not to:

    break things, or
    mistreat things.

It is best if you:

> slow down,
> try again at another time, and
> get someone to help you.

Also, it is OK to:

> cry,
> scream,
> yell,
> jump up and down, or
> hit or kick things that cannot be damaged
> (like pillows, punching bags, or beds) as long
> as you do not bother anyone else while you
> are doing it. This might mean that you need
> to go outside, or into another room and close
> the door while you are frustrated.

Anxiety is feeling worried, nervous, and upset. Anxiety is an emotion that makes people feel uncomfortable.

Pretending that you are not worried or hiding the fact that you are anxious is not a good way to handle your anxiety.

Admitting that you are nervous and talking about whatever is worrying you are good things to do when you are anxious.

THINK

Have you ever felt anxious?   Yes ☐   No ☐

List the times you were anxious:

_____

_____

_____

When was the last time you were anxious?

_____

What did you do?   How did you handle your anxiety?

_____

REMEMBER

When you are unsure of what is going to happen to you,
it is normal for you to feel anxious. But when you
do feel anxious, try not to:

pretend that you are not anxious, or
hide your true feelings.

It is best if you:

   admit that you are anxious, and
   find out and talk about whatever is worrying
      you.

Also, it is understandable for you to:

   worry about things that you do not know about, or
   worry that something is going to happen to you
      that may hurt.

Fear is feeling frightened or scared. Fear is an emotion that makes people feel uncomfortable.

But sometimes . . . fear makes a person do what needs to be done.

Acting as though you are not frightened of anything because you want people to think that you are big and brave is not a good way to handle your fear.

It's important to pay attention to your fears because they may be warning you that you are in danger. Admitting that you are afraid and being cautious are the best ways to handle your fears.

Other things to do are:

tell someone else about your fears, and ask questions and find out about them.

Sometimes you will find that you do not need to be afraid of the thing that is scaring you.

95

THINK

Have you ever been afraid?   Yes ☐   No ☐

List the things that scare you the most:

_____

_____

_____

When was the last time you were afraid?

_____

What did you do? How did you handle your fear?

_____

REMEMBER

Being afraid of things that may harm you is normal.
But when you are afraid, try not to:

act as though you aren't afraid because you want
people to think that you are big and brave.

It is best if you:

pay attention to your fears,
realize that fear is often a warning that you may be
  in danger,
admit that you are afraid,
be cautious,
tell someone else about your fear, and
ask questions and find out about the things that
  scare you.

Also, it is understandable for you to:

want to be with someone when you are afraid,
be afraid of things that you don't understand,
be afraid of things that you think might hurt you, or
want to get away and hide from things that scare you.

Disappointment is feeling letdown. Disappointment is an emotion that makes people feel uncomfortable.

THAT MARK HAS REALLY DISAPPOINTED ME THIS TIME. HE SAID HE WOULD HELP ME WITH MY PAPER ROUTE SO I WOULDN'T MISS THE BASEBALL GAME.

But sometimes . . .

disappointment makes a person do what needs to be done.

Saying mean things or getting back at the person who disappointed you is not a good way to handle disappointment.

I WAS REALLY DISAPPOINTED WHEN YOU DIDN'T COME AND HELP ME WITH MY PAPER ROUTE. WHY DIDN'T YOU COME?

I FORGOT. I'M REALLY SORRY, TOM.

Telling someone that you are disappointed, telling him or her why you are, and finding out the reasons for being letdown . . .

are good things to do when you are disappointed.

101

THINK

Have you ever been disappointed?   Yes ☐ No ☐

List some times when you were disappointed:

_____

_____

_____

When was the last time you were disappointed?

_____

What did you do? How did you handle your disappointment?

_____

REMEMBER

When someone has let you down, it is normal for you to feel disappointed. But when you are disappointed, try not to:

say mean things to the person, or
get back at the person.

It is best if you:

> tell someone that you are disappointed,
> explain why you are disappointed, and
> find out why you were let down.

Also, it is understandable for you to:

> cry,
> want to be alone,
> be angry at the person who disappointed you,
> wonder whether or not the person will let you
>   down again, or
> be afraid to trust the person until you are shown
>   that he or she will not disappoint you again.

Defeat is the feeling of losing, failing, or being beaten.
Defeat is an emotion that makes people feel uncomfortable.

But sometimes . . .

defeat makes a person do what needs to be done.

Believing that you are a loser and that you will never win, giving up, or not trying is not a good way to handle defeat.

Remembering that everyone loses once in a while and remembering that no one always wins are good ways to handle defeat. Other good things to do are: work harder, practice more, keep trying, and don't give up.

THINK

Have you ever felt defeated?   Yes ☐ No ☐

List the times you felt defeated:

_____

_____

_____

When was the last time you felt defeated?

_____

What did you do?   How did you handle defeat?

_____

REMEMBER

When you lose or fail, it is normal for you to feel defeated. But when you feel defeated, try not to:

> believe you are a loser,
> believe you will never win,
> give up, or
> stop trying.

It is best for you to:

      remember that everyone loses once in a while,
      remember that no one wins all the time,
      work harder,
      practice more,
      keep trying, and
      not give up.

Also, it is understandable for you to:

      not want to lose or fail,
      feel embarrassed about losing,
      not want others to know about your losses and
         failures,
      get discouraged, or
      want to give up.

Anger
Guilt
Jealousy
Grief
Loneliness
Rejection
Humiliation
Frustration
Anxiety
Fear
Disappointment, and
Defeat

. . . are all feelings that make people feel uncomfortable. They are feelings that make people feel bad.

List some other feelings that make people feel
uncomfortable:

_____

_____

_____

Remember, although uncomfortable feelings make
people feel bad, they can be good! Uncomfortable
feelings can be good because they can make a person
do the things that need to be done. They can also
make a person want to grow and change for the
better, and they can help a person appreciate his or
her comfortable feelings.

The key to living a happy life is to appreciate and enjoy your comfortable feelings and learn how to handle your uncomfortable feelings.

Chapter 3

Handling Your Downs

When you are feeling down, don't stay there. Do something!

Once you answer this question,

I FEEL LONELY.

you will have found out what
you are feeling. That is the
first step to handling
your downs.

After you have found out what you are feeling, ask yourself a second question.

WHY DO I FEEL LONELY?

Once you answer this question, you will have learned what is causing you to feel the way you do.

119

After you have learned what is causing you to feel the way you do, ask yourself a third question.

Once you answer this question,
you will have decided what you should do about your feelings.

After you have decided what you should do about your feelings, you need to. . .

do it.

When you are feeling down, don't stop there.
Do something about it!

So that you will not forget the four steps to handling your downs, here they are once again.

1. Find out what you are feeling. Ask yourself, "What emotion am I feeling?"
2. Learn what is causing your feeling. Ask yourself, "Why do I feel the way I do?"
3. Decide what you should do. Ask yourself, "What should I do about the way I feel?"
4. Do what you decided you should do.

Conclusion

Comfortable feelings can help you have fun and enjoy life. Uncomfortable feelings can:

> make you want to do the things that need to
>   be done,
> make you want to grow and change for the
>   better, and
> help you appreciate your comfortable feelings.

It is normal and healthy to feel both comfortable and uncomfortable feelings. That's why. . .

Every person, no matter who he or she is,
has ups and downs.